Making Their Mark: Women in Science and Medicine™

Rachel Carson
Writer and Environmentalist

Liza N. Burby

The Rosen Publishing Group's
PowerKids Press™
New York

Published in 1997 by The Rosen Publishing Group, Inc.
29 East 21st Street, New York, NY 10010

First Edition

Book Design: Erin McKenna

Photo Credits: Cover © AP/Wide World Photos; p. 4 © M. Thonig/H. Armstrong Roberts, Inc.; p. 7 © Guillermina De Ferrari; p. 8 © Archive Photos; p. 11 © W. Metzen/H. Armstrong Roberts, Inc.; p. 12 © H. Armstrong Roberts, Inc.; p. 15 © Black Mamba/H. Armstrong Roberts, Inc.; p. 16 © AP/Wide World Photos; p. 19 © P. Wallick/H. Armstrong Roberts, Inc.; p. 20 © Wide World Photos, Inc.

Burby, Liza N.
  Rachel Carson/ by Liza N. Burby
     p.   cm. — (Making their mark)
  Includes index.
  Summary: A simple presentation of the life of the biologist whose writings initiated the environmental movement.
  ISBN 0-8239-5023-9 (library bound)
  1. Carson, Rachel, 1907–1964—Juvenile literature. 2. Marine biologists—United States—Biography—Juvenile literature. 3. Environmentalists—United States—Biography—Juvenile literature. [1. Carson, Rachel, 1907–1964. 2. Science writers. 3. Biologists. 4. Environmentalists. 5. Women—Biography.] I. Title. II. Series: Burby, Liza N. Making their mark.
QH91.3.C3B87 1996
574' .092—dc20
[B]
96-41731
CIP
AC

Manufactured in the United States of America

Contents

Early Lessons

Rachel Carson was born on May 27, 1907, in Springdale, Pennsylvania. She first learned to love **nature** (NAY-chur) when she was a child. Rachel liked to explore the river and woods near her home. Her mother, Marie, often went with her. Marie taught Rachel the names of the different kinds of birds and flowers. She also taught Rachel that everything in nature has a job to do and people should not try to stop it.

► Rachel learned about different plants and animals from the woods near her home.

A Young Writer

Rachel loved to write poems and stories. When her older brother went off to fight in World War I, he sent letters to his family about what he saw. When Rachel was in fourth grade, she turned one of his letters into a story. She sent it to a **famous** (FAY-mus) magazine. The magazine **published** (PUB-lisht) her story. This made her very proud and she gained a lot of confidence. She wrote two more stories for the magazine. All three stories won awards.

Rachel liked to write stories just as this girl does. You may like to write stories, too. ▼

A Change in Plans

Rachel decided she would become a writer. But Rachel was not sure what to write about. She had always read books about nature and wildlife. When Rachel was in college, she took a **biology** (by-OL-oh-jee) class. She was so excited about learning how nature worked that she decided to become a **scientist** (SY-en-tist) instead.

▼ Rachel's love of biology and nature stayed with her throughout her life.

Rachel Sees the Ocean

One summer, Rachel worked with **marine life** (ma-REEN LYF) at a **laboratory** (LAB-ruh-tor-ee) in Massachusetts. There she saw the ocean for the first time. From then on, the ocean was an important part of her life. Because she needed money to pay for school, Rachel worked as a teacher while she studied biology at a **university** (yoon-ih-VER-sih-tee) in Maryland. She graduated in 1932.

The ocean became a very important part of Rachel's life. ▼

Something to Write About

Rachel found a job as a writer in Washington, D.C. Her job was to write radio shows about how people could **conserve** (kun-SURV), or take care of, the ocean. By becoming a **biologist** (by-OL-oh-jist), Rachel had given herself something to write about. She became an **aquatic** (ah-KWA-tik) biologist and studied the ocean. She used her knowledge of the ocean to write articles for magazines and newspapers.

▶ Rachel's radio shows taught people about the need for taking care of the ocean.

Her First Book

A book publisher thought that what Rachel had written in her articles was important. He asked her to write a book. She wrote *Under the Sea Wind*, which explains how birds and fish live together with the sea. The book was published in 1941. Readers found her ideas very interesting. Scientists also thought her work was important.

Under the Sea Wind talks about how sea animals live with the ocean. ▼

A Famous Writer

Rachel thought it was important to write books on the things she cared about. In 1951, she wrote *The Sea Around Us*. In this book, Rachel describes the many parts of the sea, from the waves down to the sea floor. People liked the book, and Rachel became famous. In 1954, Rachel wrote another book about how sea creatures live together, called *Edge of the Sea*.

▶ Rachel received many honors for her books on the ocean.

Rachel Learns About DDT

In 1958, Rachel learned that many birds had died after being sprayed with a **pesticide** (pes-tih-SYD) called DDT. It was used to kill insects that eat **crops** (KROPS). DDT was often sprayed over crops, animals, water, even children playing outdoors. Everyone thought it was harmless. But Rachel worried that DDT was hurting people and animals. She started to study the effects of DDT. In 1962, her book *Silent Spring* was published. This book told the world how pesticides hurt the earth and people.

Rachel believed that pesticides were harmful, and wanted to do something about it. ▶

Anger About _Silent Spring_

Many people were angry about Rachel's book. The people who made DDT called her a liar. They were afraid of losing their businesses. Farmers wondered what they could use instead of DDT to stop insects from hurting their crops. Rachel appeared on TV to talk about what she had discovered. U.S. President John F. Kennedy chose a special group of people to study DDT. In 1963, the group reported that what Rachel had written in _Silent Spring_ was correct.

▶ After reading _Silent Spring_, people tried harder to take care of the world around them.

A Lesson About Nature

Rachel Carson was a **courageous** (koh-RAY-jus) woman who stood up for her beliefs. Her book changed the way people treat the **environment** (en-VY-ron-ment). When Rachel died in 1964, laws were already being passed to protect the environment. The U.S. Environmental Protection Agency was formed in 1970 to make sure that we take care of nature. Since 1972, it has been against the law to use DDT. Rachel taught the world that we must protect nature or we could destroy it.

Glossary

aquatic (ah-KWA-tik) Having to do with water.

biologist (by-OL-oh-jist) A person who studies biology.

biology (by-OL-oh-jee) The study of living things.

conserve (kun-SURV) To protect something from harm.

courageous (koh-RAY-jus) Being brave.

crop (KROP) Food grown to eat or to sell at markets.

environment (en-VY-ron-ment) The place in which plants, animals, and humans live.

famous (FAY-mus) Well known.

laboratory (LAB-ruh-tor-ee) Place where a scientist works.

marine life (ma-REEN LYF) Animals that live in and around the ocean.

nature (NAY-chur) The world of living things.

pesticide (pes-tih-SYD) A poison used to kill insects.

publish (PUB-lish) To print a book or article.

scientist (SY-en-tist) A person who studies the way things are and act in the universe.

university (yoon-ih-VER-sih-tee) A large school that students go to after high school.

Index